LEON KIRCHNER

PIANO SONATA NO. 3
"THE FORBIDDEN"

commissioned by the Joel Fan Foundation
(www.joelfanmusic.com)

A recording by Joel Fan
is available on the album
Leon Kirchner: Works for Solo Piano
TROY906

duration circa 9 minutes

AMP 8327
First Printing: April 2023
ISBN: 978-1-5400-9171-0

Associated Music Publishers, Inc.

DISTRIBUTED BY

7777 W. BLUEMOUND RD. P.O. BOX 13819 MILWAUKEE, WI 53213
halleonard.com
wisemusicclassical.com

for Joel Fan

PIANO SONATA No. 3
"The Forbidden"

Leon Kirchner

4

10

poco più mosso

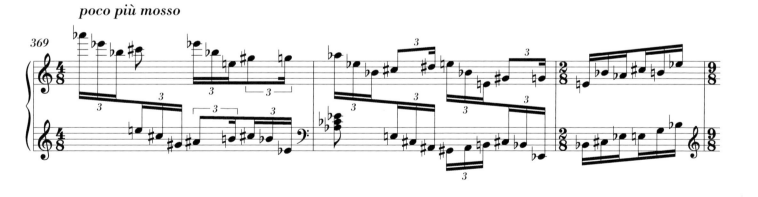